Gifted & Tal

Science
Questions & Answers
DINOSAURS
For Ages 6–8

By Barbara Saffer, Ph.D.

Interior illustrations by Neal Yamamoto

Cover illustration by Kerry Manwaring

LOWELL HOUSE JUVENILE

LOS ANGELES

NTC/Contemporary Publishing Group

For Tracey, Lyssa, Brandon, and
Chelsea, who light up our lives
—B.S.

Published by Lowell House
A division of NTC/Contemporary Publishing Group, Inc.
4255 West Touhy Avenue, Lincolnwood (Chicago), Illinois 60712 U.S.A.

Managing Director and Publisher: Jack Artenstein
Director of Publishing Services: Rena Copperman
Editorial Director: Brenda Pope-Ostrow
Director of Art Production: Bret Perry
Senior Educational Editor: Linda Gorman
Designer: Victor Perry

Lowell House books can be purchased at special discounts
when ordered in bulk for premiums and special sales.
Please contact Customer Service at:
NTC/Contemporary Publishing Group
4255 W. Touhy Avenue
Lincolnwood, IL 60712
1-800-323-4900

Printed and bound in the United States of America

Library of Congress Catalog Card Number: 99-76528

ISBN: 0-7373-0348-4

ML 10 9 8 7 6 5 4 3 2 1

Note to Parents

Teach a child facts and you give her knowledge. Teach her to think and you give her wisdom. This is the principle behind the entire series of *Gifted & Talented*® materials. And this is the reason that thinking skills are being stressed in classrooms throughout the country.

The questions and answers in the **Gifted & Talented**® **Question & Answer** books have been designed specifically to promote the development of critical and creative thinking skills. Each page features one "topic question" that is answered above a corresponding picture. This topic provides the springboard to the following questions on the page.

Each of these six related questions focuses on a different higher-level thinking skill. The skills include knowledge and recall, comprehension, deduction, inference, sequencing, prediction, classification, analyzing, problem solving, and creative expansion.

The topic question, answer, and artwork contain the answers or clues to the answers for some of the other questions. Certain questions, however, can only be answered by relating the topic to other facts that your child may already know. At the back of the book are suggested answers to help you guide your child.

Effective questioning has been used to develop a child's intellectual gifts since the time of Socrates. Certainly, it is the most common teaching technique in classrooms today. But asking questions isn't as easy as it looks! On the following page you will find a few tips to keep in mind that will help you and your child use this book more effectively.

★ First of all, let your child flip through the book and select the questions and pictures that interest him or her. If the child wants to do only one page, that's fine. If he or she wants to answer only some of the questions on a page, save the others for another time.

★ Give your child time to think! Wait at least 10 seconds before you offer any help. You'd be surprised how little time many parents and teachers give a child to think before jumping right in and answering a question themselves.

★ Help your child by restating or rephrasing the question if necessary. But again, make sure you pause and give the child time to answer first. Also, don't ask the same question over and over! Go on to another question, or use hints to prompt your child when needed.

★ Encourage your child to give more details or expand upon answers by asking questions such as "What made you say that?" or "Why do you think so?"

★ This book will not only teach your child about many things, but it will teach *you* a lot about your child. Make the most of your time together—and have fun!

The answers at the back of the book are to be used as a guide. Sometimes your child may come up with an answer that is different but still a good answer. Remember, the principle behind all *Gifted & Talented*® materials is to **teach your child to think**—not just to give answers.

What kind of animal were dinosaurs?

Dinosaurs were reptiles that lived millions of years ago. Like other reptiles, dinosaurs laid eggs, and had backbones, lungs, and scaly skin. Two features help scientists identify dinosaurs: dinosaur skulls have two holes behind the eye sockets, and certain bones in dinosaur hips resemble those of lizards or birds. Dinosaurs lived on land and walked with their legs under their bodies, not out to the sides like alligators. Many different kinds of dinosaurs lived all over the world.

1. What are some features of reptiles?
2. Can you name some living reptiles?
3. Which living reptile do you think looks most like a dinosaur?
4. Can you name some other animals that walk with their legs under their bodies?
5. What are some ways that having legs under your body is more useful than having them out to the sides?
6. Dinosaur characters, such as Barney and Littlefoot, are very popular. What's your favorite dinosaur character? Why?

Where did dinosaurs come from?

Scientists believe the ancestors of dinosaurs *evolved*, or developed, from amphibians. Amphibians, such as frogs and salamanders, can live on land. However, they must keep their skin wet and return to water to lay eggs. Amphibians that

Thecodontosaurus

lived long ago looked like big salamanders. Over millions of years, some of them developed into animals with stronger skeletons, tougher skins, and hard eggs. These new animals were the first reptiles. One ancient group of reptiles, called *thecodonts* (THEE-koh-donts), were slim and fast. In time, they evolved into dinosaurs.

1. What are some living amphibians?
2. What does **ancient** mean?
3. How did some ancient amphibians develop into reptiles?
4. Where do you think amphibians came from?
5. How many words can you make up with the letters in **amphibian**?
6. Do you think it's easier to live in water or on land? Why?

What were the two main groups of dinosaurs?

Dinosaurs are divided into two main groups, based on the arrangement of their hipbones. The Ornithischia (or-nih-THIS-kee-ah) were the bird-hipped dinosaurs.

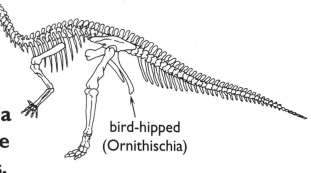

bird-hipped
(Ornithischia)

Their two lower hipbones were close together and pointed backward. The Saurischia (saw-RIS-kee-ah) were the lizard-hipped dinosaurs. Their two lower hipbones were separated, with one pointed forward and the other pointed backward. The Ornithischia included only plant-eaters. The Saurischia included both plant-eaters and meat-eaters.

lizard-hipped
(Saurischia)

1. Which dinosaurs had hipbones that were close together?
2. Where are your hips? Point to them.
3. Which group of dinosaurs would Tyrannosaurus (ty-RAN-oh-SAWR-us), a meat-eater, be in?
4. Can you name some living animals that are plant-eaters?
5. Can you name some living animals that are meat-eaters?
6. Do you think human beings are more similar to birds or lizards? Why?

When were dinosaurs first discovered?

The first dinosaur teeth were discovered by rock quarry workers in England in the early 1820s. The workers brought the teeth to Dr. Gideon Mantell, a fossil collector, who thought they came from a huge lizard that no longer existed. Because the teeth resembled iguana teeth, Dr. Mantell named the animal *Iguanodon* (ih-GWAN-oh-don), which means "iguana tooth." Around the same time, Professor William Buckland described an animal called *Megalosaurus* (MEG-ah-lo-SAWR-us), which means "big lizard." Scientists later discovered that Iguanodon was a plant-eating dinosaur and Megalosaurus was a meat-eating dinosaur.

1. Why did the quarry workers take the bones to Dr. Mantell?
2. Do you think you would recognize dinosaur teeth in a rock quarry? What do you think they would look like?

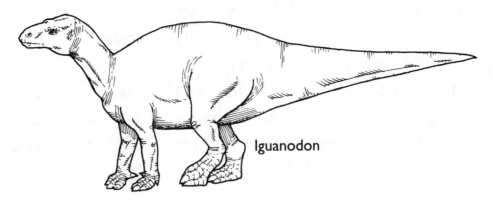

Iguanodon

3. Why do you think some dinosaur arm bones and leg bones have teeth marks?

4. Why do you think dinosaurs were originally called lizards?

5. Many dinosaur fossils are found on private ranches or farms. If you discovered dinosaur fossils in your backyard, what would you do with them?

6. People are always trying to discover new things. Why do you think this is?

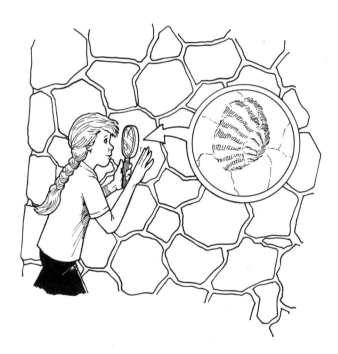

One Step Further

Rocks are found in many places, including parks, walls of buildings, and statues. Ask an adult to accompany you to some buildings whose walls are made of rocks, such as schools, libraries, and office buildings. Examine the rocks with a magnifying glass. Can you find fossils, such as shells or bones, in the rocks?

What are scientists who study dinosaurs called?

Scientists who study *fossils,* or the remains of ancient plants and animals, are called *paleontologists* (PAY-lee-un-TAHL-oh-jists). Dinosaur paleontologists search for dinosaur fossils all over the world. When they discover dinosaur remains, paleontologists make notes about their find and map the area. Then they carefully remove the fossils, pack them in plaster jackets, and take them to laboratories for study.

1. Do all paleontologists study dinosaurs?
2. Why do you think some paleontologists fought over dinosaur fossils?
3. What do you think plant fossils look like?
4. What kinds of tools do you think paleontologists use?
5. Why do paleontologists make notes and maps when they find dinosaur fossils?
6. If a paleontologist came to your classroom for Career Day, what would you ask her or him?

Who made up the word *dinosaur*?

When people first found dinosaur fossils, they thought the huge bones came from giants or dragons. After a while, scientists realized the bones came from real animals that had once lived on Earth but no longer existed. In 1842, Sir Richard Owen, a British scientist, named this group of animals *Dinosauria* (DY-no-SAWR-ee-ah), which means "terrible lizards." People immediately became fascinated by dinosaurs.

1. How tall do you think a giant would be?
2. How many years ago was 1842?
3. If you had discovered and named dinosaurs, what would you have called them?
4. The first dinosaur drawings looked more like giant mammals than dinosaurs. Why do you think this is?
5. When scientists put together dinosaur skeletons, they sometimes use the wrong skulls by mistake. Why do you think this happens?
6. Pretend you've found the remains of creatures even more fascinating than dinosaurs. What would these creatures be? Draw a picture of them on a separate piece of paper.

How long ago did dinosaurs live?

The history of Earth is divided into *eras,* or time periods. Dinosaurs lived during the Mesozoic (MEH-suh-ZOH-ik) Era, which is also called the *Age of Reptiles.* The Mesozoic Era began 245 million years ago and ended 65 million years ago. It is divided into three *periods*—the Triassic (try-AH-sik), Jurassic (juh-RAH-sik), and Cretaceous (kreh-TAY-shus). The landscape and vegetation of the Earth changed from one period to another, and dinosaur life changed as well.

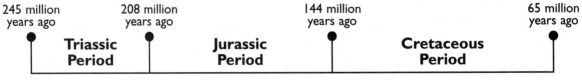

245 million years ago · 208 million years ago · 144 million years ago · 65 million years ago

Triassic Period · **Jurassic Period** · **Cretaceous Period**

M E S O Z O I C E R A

1. What was the Age of Reptiles?
2. Do you think the first dinosaurs were large or small? What do you think they ate?
3. How long did the Mesozoic Era last?
4. Dinosaurs are *prehistoric* animals. What does that mean?
5. The era we live in is called the *Cenozoic* (SEE-nuh-ZOH-ik) *Era.* Why do you think it's sometimes called the *Age of Mammals?*
6. If you had a time machine that could take you back to the Mesozoic Era, would you go? Why or why not?

Where did dinosaurs live?

When dinosaurs first appeared, Earth's continents were all joined together as one "supercontinent" called *Pangaea* (pan-JEE-uh). Dinosaurs roamed all over the giant landmass. When Pangaea began to split into separate continents, about 150 million years ago, dinosaurs traveled with the moving continents. As a result, dinosaurs lived on every landmass on Earth.

Pangaea
(about 250 million years ago)

Pangaea splitting
(about 150 million years ago)

1. What was Pangaea?
2. What do you think surrounded Pangaea?
3. How many continents are there on Earth? Do you know their names?
4. Which continent is the largest? Which one is the smallest?
5. Do you think the continents are moving now?
6. Do you think all of Pangaea had the same weather conditions? Why or why not?

What was the world like when dinosaurs lived?

The world's *climate,* or long-term weather, was generally warm during the Mesozoic (MEH-suh-ZOH-ik) Era—the time when dinosaurs lived. In the early Mesozoic, there were many conifer trees and ferns. Later, gingko trees appeared. These were followed by flowering plants, which added flecks of color to the Earth. Just like today's Earth, some places in the Mesozoic world had tropical rain forests, and others had sandy deserts or great plains. Different kinds of dinosaurs lived in each of these habitats.

1. What was the climate like when dinosaurs lived?
2. What is the climate like where you live? If dinosaurs were still living, do you think they would do well in your climate?
3. Do you think the North Pole and South Pole were covered with ice when dinosaurs were alive?
4. How does climate affect plants?
5. What is a habitat?
6. Flowering plants produce seeds inside fruits. How does this help the plants spread to new places?

Were there any people when dinosaurs lived?

No. Dinosaurs lived long before people appeared on Earth. However, human beings' distant ancestors, the first *primates,* appeared at the end of the dinosaur age. The first primates were similar to tree shrews. They were squirrel-size animals, with pointed noses, long tails, and sharp claws. Over many millions of years, these early primates *evolved,* or developed, into advanced primates—monkeys, then apes, then humans. The first humans appeared about 5 million years ago.

evolution of primates

1. Did dinosaurs ever eat people?
2. What is an ancestor? Who are your family's ancestors?
3. What do you think early shrewlike primates ate?
4. Which of these animals are primates: baboons, squirrels, gorillas, orangutans, bears, raccoons?
5. Advanced primates, such as chimpanzees, can use simple tools. What do you think a chimpanzee might do with a stick?
6. What are some features of humans today that make them such successful animals?

What are fossils?

Fossils are the remains or traces of plants and animals that lived long ago. The main way fossils form is when the hard parts of animals—such as shells, bones, and teeth—are buried for millions of years. Water that contains lots of minerals seeps into the remains, and hard minerals replace the original parts. The remains turn to stone and are preserved. Most fossils form deep underground. They are exposed when the overlying rock wears away or is pushed up to form mountains. *Trace fossils* don't include any plant or animal remains. They are evidence, however, that a living thing existed. Trace fossils include preserved skin impressions, nests, footprints, leaf prints, animal burrows, and animal droppings.

1. What does **preserve** mean?
2. Is a bone from a raccoon that died last year a fossil?

3. How long do you think it takes to remove a dinosaur fossil from the surrounding rock?

4. When scientists find dinosaur footprints, how do they know which dinosaurs made them?

5. What can scientists learn about a dinosaur from its *dung*, or droppings?

6. Imagine you took pictures of your room and sent them to a pen pal far away. What could the pen pal learn about you from the pictures?

One Step Further

Make your own trace fossils. Get a container of Play-Doh, a piece of wax paper, and a rolling pin. Put the wax paper on a flat surface. Divide the Play-Doh into two equal chunks. Roll one chunk into a ball and put it on the wax paper. Flatten it with the rolling pin until it's a sheet about ⅛-inch thick. Do the same with the other chunk of Play-Doh. Press your hand onto one sheet of Play-Doh and your foot onto the other. Leave the Play-Doh for several days, until it dries and hardens. When it does, you will have "trace fossils" of your hand and foot. Use the same steps to make trace fossils of other things, such as leaves, pet paw prints, and pine cones.

Where do scientists look for dinosaur fossils?

Scientists look for dinosaur fossils all over the world. Most fossils are found in *sedimentary* rocks. Sedimentary rocks are made from layers of *sediments*—mud, sand, and gravel—that harden into stone. When dinosaurs died, their remains were sometimes covered with windblown sand, or washed into rivers or lakes. If the remains were quickly covered with sediments, the bones were preserved. As the sediments hardened into rock, the bones became fossils.

1. Where could you go to see dinosaur fossils?
2. How do you think dinosaur bones were washed into rivers and lakes?
3. What do you think sandstone is made of?
4. Why do you think dinosaur bones had to be covered with sediments to become fossils?
5. What is happening to the dinosaur in the picture? Will this dinosaur's bones become fossils?
6. Pretend you're a scientist in charge of a fossil-hunting expedition. Where will you go? Who will you take? What will you bring?

How are dinosaurs named?

Names for new animals are usually created from Latin or Greek words. Giganotosaurus (jig-ah-**NOT**-oh-**SAWR**-us), for example, was a huge dinosaur found in South America. Its name comes from the Greek words *gigas* (giant), *notos* (south), and *sauros* (lizard). Dinosaurs can also be named for people. Zuniceratops christopheri (**ZOO**-nee-**SER**-ah-tops kris-**TOF**-er-eye), found in New Mexico, was named for the Zuni Indians and for nine-year-old Christopher Wolfe, who helped discover the fossils.

1. What languages are usually used to name new animals?
2. Have you ever given a name to things, like pets, toys, or bicycles? How did you pick the names?
3. Albertosaurus (al-**BUHR**-tuh-**SAWR**-us) was named for the province in Canada where its fossils were found. What province was it named for?
4. Can you find New Mexico on a map? What states are around it?
5. Do you think a dinosaur, like Tyrannosaurus rex, has different names in different countries?
6. If a dinosaur were named after you, what would you want it to be called?

How do scientists know how big dinosaurs were?

After paleontologists dig up a dinosaur's bones, they rebuild the skeleton. The skeleton shows them the size and shape of the dinosaur. All *vertebrates,* or animals with backbones, have similar skeletons. That's why scientists study modern animals to learn how to reconstruct dinosaurs. A vertebrate's backbone, for example, is made up of a series of bones called *vertebrae* (VER-tuh-bray). The skull goes on the front of the backbone and the tail goes on the back. Scientists also examine modern animals to figure out what the soft parts of dinosaurs—like muscles, organs, and skin—looked like.

1. What are vertebrates?
2. Run your hand down your backbone. What do your vertebrae feel like?
3. *Invertebrates* are animals without backbones. Can you name some invertebrates?

Apatosaurus grew up to 70 feet long

4. How do you think paleontologists attach the bones of a dinosaur skeleton together?

5. Do you think it was better to be a large dinosaur or a small dinosaur? Why?

6. Scientists rarely find complete skeletons of dinosaurs. How do you think they fill in the missing parts?

One Step Further

Reconstruct a dinosaur skeleton. Make a copy of this page on a copy machine. Get scissors, a sheet of dark construction paper, and a glue stick. Cut the dinosaur bones out of the copied page. Using the cat skeleton as a guide, try to "reconstruct" the dinosaur skeleton by gluing the dinosaur bones onto the construction paper. How is the dinosaur skeleton similar to the cat skeleton? How is it different?

How do scientists know how dinosaurs moved?

Paleontologists figure out how dinosaurs moved by studying their bones. *Muscle scars* on dinosaur bones show where muscles were attached to the bones, and how big they were. Strong bones and larger muscles were needed for running and fighting. Studying *joints,* the places where bones come together, gives scientists an idea of how an animal's body could bend and turn. Paleontologists also study muscles in relatives of dinosaurs, such as crocodiles and birds. Using all this information, scientists "reconstruct" dinosaurs and figure out how they moved.

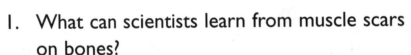

muscle scars

1. What can scientists learn from muscle scars on bones?
2. Which muscles do you think are larger, your arm muscles or your leg muscles?
3. Which joints give you more movement, your wrist joints or your elbow joints?
4. Why do you think dinosaur bones used for running and fighting were very strong?
5. Why can't scientists study dinosaur muscles?
6. Some kinds of animals don't form fossils. Why?

What was dinosaur skin like?

Dinosaur skin impressions are sometimes preserved in rocks. They show that most dinosaurs had tough, scaly, waterproof skin, like other reptiles. Polacanthus (pol-ah-KAN-thus) was an armored plant-eater. It had bumpy skin, with bony spikes and plates for extra protection. Meat-eaters such as Carnotaurus (KAR-no-TAWR-us) had smooth scales, like a lizard's. Some small meat-eaters may have had feathers, like birds. Dinosaur skin color is not preserved. However, scientists believe that dinosaurs had various patterns and colors, just like today's reptiles.

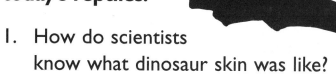

1. How do scientists know what dinosaur skin was like?
2. Can you name some things that are made from animal skin?
3. Why do you think armored plant-eaters had tougher skin than big meat-eaters?
4. What does **waterproof** mean?
5. How does waterproof skin help animals that live on land?
6. Can you name animals that use their colors or patterns to attract mates? to scare off enemies? to hide themselves?

Were dinosaurs warm-blooded or cold-blooded?

Warm-blooded animals, like mammals and birds, make enough heat from their body processes to keep their body temperature high. They can be active all the time. *Cold-blooded* animals, like crocodiles and frogs, don't make

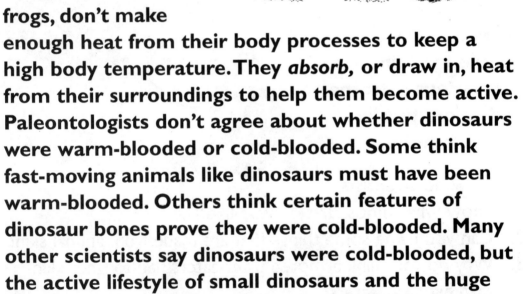

enough heat from their body processes to keep a high body temperature. They *absorb,* or draw in, heat from their surroundings to help them become active. Paleontologists don't agree about whether dinosaurs were warm-blooded or cold-blooded. Some think fast-moving animals like dinosaurs must have been warm-blooded. Others think certain features of dinosaur bones prove they were cold-blooded. Many other scientists say dinosaurs were cold-blooded, but the active lifestyle of small dinosaurs and the huge size of big dinosaurs "kept them warm."

1. Which animal in the picture would be more active in cold weather? Why?
2. Can you name some warm-blooded animals? some cold-blooded animals?

3. Warm-blooded animals need much more food than cold-blooded animals. Why do you think this is?
4. The Earth's climate was very warm when dinosaurs lived. How would this have helped cold-blooded animals?
5. Scientists think some dinosaurs might have hibernated during the winter. What modern animals hibernate?
6. Warm-blooded animals are called *endotherms,* which means "heat from within." What do you think **ectotherms** are? What do you think **ectotherm** means?

One Step Further

You will need an adult's help for this activity. Find out which stays warmer longer, a big object or a small object. Get a large baking potato (about 6 inches long), a small baking potato (about 3 inches long), a microwave-safe plate, a fork, a knife, and an oven mitt. Poke holes all around each potato with the fork. Poke the large potato about 10 times and the small potato about 5 times. Place the potatoes on the microwave-safe plate, and put the plate into a microwave oven. Heat the potatoes on high power for 15 minutes. Use the oven mitt to remove the plate from the oven. Wait 15 minutes, then cut the potatoes in half. Touch the cut surface of each potato with your finger. Which is warmer? Why?

What kind of teeth did dinosaurs have?

Meat-eating dinosaurs had sharp, curved teeth. Tyrannosaurus (ty-RAN-oh-SAWR-us), for example, had many thick, pointed teeth with sawlike edges. The teeth, as long as steak knives, easily ripped chunks of meat from the animals it ate. Plant-eating dinosaurs had various kinds of teeth.

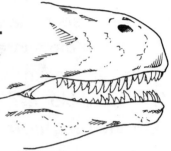

meat-eater's teeth
(Tyrannosaurus)

Diplodocus (dih-PLOD-oh-kus), for example, had a small number of sticklike teeth for raking vegetation, which it swallowed whole. Duck-billed dinosaurs, on the other hand, had numerous grinding teeth, to chew up tough plants.

1. Which kind of dinosaur had very sharp teeth?
2. How many teeth do you have?
3. What do you do with a baby tooth when it falls out?

plant-eater's teeth
(Diplodocus)

4. How do you think a dog's teeth matches its food? a horse's teeth? your teeth?
5. Why should you always chew your food before you swallow it?
6. If you were an animal dentist at a zoo, how would you fix the teeth of a big tiger? a tiny bat?

How smart were dinosaurs?

To figure out how smart a dinosaur was, paleontologists compare the size of its brain to the size of its body. Scientists think dinosaurs that had large brains compared to their bodies were smart. Small, nimble meat-eaters, like Troodon (TROH-oh-don) and Oviraptor (OH-vih-RAP-tor), had big brains. Both guarded their eggs, and scientists think they were among the smartest dinosaurs. Giant long-necks, like Brachiosaurus (BRAK-ee-oh-SAWR-us), had rather small brains. They probably walked slowly and performed only simple activities.

Troodon

1. Why do scientists think some dinosaurs were fairly smart?
2. Do you think any dinosaurs were as smart as people?
3. What living animals are thought to be very smart?
4. What kinds of things do you think baby dinosaurs might have learned from their parents?
5. What are some things people do to make themselves smarter?
6. Think of some people you know. Do you think they're smart? Why?

Why did some huge dinosaurs have tiny heads?

Diplodocus (dih-PLOD-oh-kus) and other long-necks had big bodies and long necks. Their heads, however, were small. This was probably because the animals' slender necks couldn't support big, heavy skulls. For many years, paleontologists thought all long-necks lifted their heads high, to feed on treetops. But recently scientists found that Diplodocus may not have been able to lift its head high after all. It may have grazed on low-lying plants instead.

Mamenchisaurus

1. What does **slender** mean?
2. Can you name some living animals with long necks?
3. Can you name some living animals with short necks?
4. Scientists think dinosaurs grew for their whole lives. Do humans grow for their whole lives?
5. Some long-necked dinosaurs were taller than three-story buildings. Would you like to ride on the head of an animal this tall? Why or why not?
6. Do you think huge animals like long-necks lived in muddy swamps or on dry land? Explain your answer.

Why did some dinosaurs have armor plates?

Some plant-eating dinosaurs, called *ankylosaurs* (ANG-kih-loh-sawrs), had hard scales and bony plates. This armor protected them from the bites and claws of meat-eaters. Ankylosaurus (ANG-kih-loh-SAWR-us), for example, was covered with thick plates and bony studs, which a predator couldn't bite through. It also had a bony club on its tail that it could use as a weapon. Some other ankylosaurs were protected by helmets, spikes, or horns.

Daspletosaurus

Ankylosaurus

1. What is happening in the picture?
2. Triceratops (try-SAYR-ah-tops) wasn't an ankylosaur, but it had long horns on its head. What do you think it used its horns for?
3. What are some living animals that have horns?
4. What are some living animals that have natural armor?
5. How did armor suits protect knights of long ago?
6. Some small plant-eaters had no horns or armor. How do you think they avoided being eaten by predators?

What did dinosaurs use their tails for?

Plant-eating dinosaurs used their tails to defend themselves. Long-necks, like Diplodocus (dih-PLOD-oh-kus), had whiplike tails which they used to lash out at meat-eaters. They also used their tails for balance when they walked. Armored dinosaurs had dangerous tails. For example, Stegosaurus's (STEG-oh-SAWR-us) tail had spikes as long as baseball bats. When slammed into a predator, its tail would have caused serious injury. Some nimble meat-eaters, like Deinonychus (dy-NON-ih-kus), probably used their tails for balance when they ran.

Diplodocus

Stegosaurus

Deinonychus

1. How did some dinosaurs protect themselves with their tails?
2. Why did dinosaurs need long tails to balance their bodies?
3. What do you think modern reptiles, like crocodiles, use their tails for?
4. How is a monkey's tail different from a crocodile's tail? What do monkeys use their tails for?
5. What do you think an airplane tail does?
6. What is the difference between a **tail** and a **tale**?

What did dinosaurs use their claws for?

Predators like Utahraptor (YOO-tah-RAP-tor) used the huge, knifelike claws on their hands and feet to kill prey. The crocodile-jawed Baryonyx (BAR-ee-ON-iks) may have used its enormous thumb claws to scoop fish out of the water, for food. Most plant-eating dinosaurs, like Iguanodon (ih-GWAN-oh-don), used their broad, flat claws to dig up plants and to strike out at attackers.

Iguanodon

Tyrannosaurus

Baryonyx

Deinonychus

1. What did meat-eating dinosaurs use their claws for?
2. Can you name some modern animals that have dangerous claws?
3. What parts of the human body are most like the claws of dinosaurs?
4. Can you name some living predators, or meat-eaters, that have no claws? How do they catch prey?
5. Where do you think Utahraptor was discovered?
6. What are some words that rhyme with **claw**? Can you make up a poem about dinosaurs using these words?

Did dinosaurs have good eyesight?

Scientists study a dinosaur's skull to figure out how big different parts of its brain were. Large "sight areas" in the brain mean the dinosaur had good eyesight. Leaellynasaura (lee-EL-in-ah-SAWR-ah) was a plant-eater from Australia. It had sharp vision, perhaps to help it see in the dark. Velociraptor (vuh-LOS-ih-RAP-tor) and Oviraptor (OH-vih-RAP-tor) also had good vision, and may have hunted at night. Not all dinosaurs had good eyesight. Some plant-eating dinosaurs had better smell than vision.

Oviraptor

1. Did all plant-eaters have good eyesight?
2. How do some people improve their eyesight?
3. Elephants have poor eyesight. How do you think they find food and detect enemies?
4. What modern animals see well in the dark?
5. Sight is one of our five senses. Can you name the other four?
6. What do people and animals use their senses for?

Did dinosaurs make sounds?

Skull bones show that many dinosaurs made sounds. Young dinosaurs may have squeaked and squealed, and older dinosaurs may have croaked, barked, or roared. The skulls of some duck-billed dinosaurs have fan-shaped or tube-shaped *crests,* or tops. Paleontologists think these crests may have been echo chambers that helped the dinosaurs make sounds. Duckbills may have bellowed to attract mates, like modern moose do.

Corythosaurus

1. What is an echo? Can you use your voice to create an echo?
2. Why do you think baby dinosaurs squealed?
3. Why do you think adult dinosaurs roared or made other noises?
4. Can you name a modern animal that roars? one that howls? one that hisses?
5. Some meat-eating dinosaurs had good hearing. How do you think this helped them?
6. What are some sounds you like? What are some sounds you don't like? Why?

How did dinosaurs reproduce?

Dinosaurs laid eggs in nests on the ground. Small dinosaurs, like Oviraptor (OH-vih-RAP-tor), may have sat on their eggs until they hatched. Many dinosaurs, however, probably covered their eggs with sand and plants to keep them warm. Dinosaur eggs ranged in size from golf balls to footballs. Eggs couldn't be too large and thick because air had to get in and babies had to break out. That's why some scientists think giant dinosaurs may have given birth to live young as big as adult pigs.

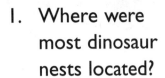

Oviraptor

1. Where were most dinosaur nests located?
2. Why do you think many dinosaurs didn't sit on their eggs to hatch them?
3. Can you name some modern animals that lay eggs?
4. Can you name some modern animals that give birth to live young? Is this better than laying eggs?
5. What are some ways to cook eggs? If you cooked a giant dinosaur egg, how many people do you think it would feed?
6. Scientists sometimes find fossilized dinosaur eggs with babies inside. What do you think they learn from these eggs?

Did dinosaurs take care of their young?

Scientists think some dinosaurs just covered their eggs and walked away. But other dinosaurs probably protected their eggs and cared for their young. Fossilized nests of Maiasaura (MAY-ah-SAWR-ah), a plant-eating duckbill, contain the fossils of many helpless baby dinosaurs. Paleontologists think one or both parents protected these youngsters and brought them food. Other baby dinosaurs hatched with well-developed legs. Scientists believe these youngsters left the nest as soon as they hatched to find their own plants to eat.

Maiasaura

1. What is happening in the picture?
2. How did your parents take care of you when you were a baby?
3. *Maiasaura* means "good mother lizard." Why do you think scientists chose this name?
4. A baby horse is called a *foal*. Can you name some other baby animals?
5. What kinds of baby animals do you like best? Why?
6. If you were teaching dinosaurs to be good parents, what would you tell them?

Did dinosaurs live alone or in groups?

Paleontologists think many plant-eating dinosaurs lived in groups, to protect themselves from predators. Evidence for this is seen in fossil beds containing many duck-billed Maiasaura (MAY-ah-SAWR-ah), both young and adult. Clusters of fossil bones from some meat-eaters, like Coelophysis (SEEL-oh-FY-sis), show that they formed groups also. Other meat-eaters may have formed temporary packs, for hunting. But many predatory dinosaurs, like the ferocious Carnotaurus (KAR-no-TAWR-us), hunted alone.

Coelophysis dinosaurs

1. When do you like to be with a group of people? When do you like to be alone?
2. Do you think plant-eating dinosaurs or meat-eating dinosaurs were more likely to live in groups? Why?
3. What are some modern animals that live in groups?
4. A group of cows is called a *herd*. What are some other animal group names?
5. Some dinosaur trails have small and large footprints close together. What do you think this shows?
6. People sometimes form groups called *clubs*. If you formed a dinosaur fan club, what would you call it?

Did dinosaurs migrate?

Paleontologists believe some dinosaurs *migrated*, or traveled from place to place, in search of food. An example of this is the large, horned plant-eater Pachyrhinosaurus (pak-ee-RINE-oh-SAWR-us). Its bones have been found in the Arctic, Alaska, and Canada. Arctic winters were long and dark in the Mesozoic Era, just like today. Plants would have died off. Scientists think Arctic dinosaurs may have migrated south in winter and north in spring to have a steady supply of food.

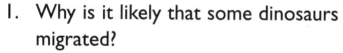

migration route of
Pachyrhinosaurus

1. Why is it likely that some dinosaurs migrated?
2. Why do some birds migrate south in winter?
3. How do migrating animals know which way to go?
4. How do maps help people when they travel?
5. Scientists believe that early humans often moved from place to place. Why do you think they did this?
6. If you lived in the Arctic, what would you do for fun during the long, dark winters?

Could dinosaurs run fast?

Some dinosaurs ran very fast, probably to escape from predators or chase prey. All swift dinosaurs had small bodies, slender tails, short arms, and long legs. To determine how fast a dinosaur moved, paleontologists measure the length of its legs compared to the rest of its body. They also measure the dinosaur's *stride,* or the distance between its footprints. The faster the dinosaur, the longer its stride. One of the fastest dinosaurs was the plant-eating Hypsilophodon (hip-sih-LOF-oh-don). It was about 6 feet long and ran at speeds of 30 miles per hour. Giant long-necks probably strolled along at about 2 miles per hour. Even long-necks, though, probably moved quickly for short distances when they needed to.

Deinonychus

Hypsilophodon

1. Why did some dinosaurs run fast?

2. Do you think you could win a race against a fast dinosaur?

3. Can you name some modern animals that run fast?

4. How far could Hypsilophodon travel in half an hour?

5. How do you think slow-moving animals, like snails and sea urchins, avoid being eaten by enemies?

6. What are some words that mean **fast**? Can you use each one in a sentence?

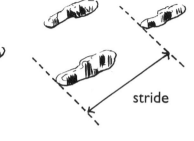

stride

One Step Further

Find out if your walking stride is different from your running stride. Get a tape measure, a paper, and a pencil. Wet the bottoms of your shoes and walk across a paved area. Your shoes will leave footprints. Measure your *stride*. This is the distance between the back of one footprint and the back of the next footprint *made by the same foot*. (For example, measure the distance between the back of one *right* footprint and the back of the next *right* footprint.) Write down the distance. Then wet the bottoms of your shoes again and run across the same area. Measure your stride again. Write down the distance. Are your two strides the same?

?

What was the smallest dinosaur?

Compsognathus (**KOMP**-sog-**NAY**-thus) was one of the smallest known dinosaurs. This meat-eater was about as big as a turkey and weighed about as much as a newborn human baby. Scientists think Compsognathus was a fast runner that chased down small lizards and other prey. Heterodontosaurus (**HET**-er-oh-**DONT**-oh-**SAWR**-us), also about as big as a turkey, was among the smallest known plant-eaters. It had several kinds of teeth, which it may have used to bite, tear, and grind plants.

Compsognathus

1. Do you think you could have lifted up Compsognathus?
2. *Heterodontosaurus* means "different tooth lizard." Why do you think scientists chose this name?
3. What is the smallest animal you ever saw?
4. Can you think of some other words that mean **small**?
5. Do you think a small dinosaur would make a good pet? Why?
6. Can you make up a story that starts, "Yesterday, I shrank to the size of a mouse"? On a separate piece of paper, draw a picture to go with your story.

What was the biggest dinosaur?

The biggest known meat-eating dinosaur was Giganotosaurus (jig-ah-**NOT**-oh-**SAWR**-us), from Argentina. Giganotosaurus measured 45 feet in length—as long as three cars—and weighed 8 tons, or slightly more than an African elephant. It walked on two legs and had long, sharp teeth. The largest known plant-eating dinosaur was the four-legged long-neck Argentinosaurus (AR-jen-**TEEN**-oh-**SAWR**-us), also from Argentina. It measured 115 feet in length—almost as long as eight cars—and weighed 100 tons, or as much as 14 African elephants.

Argentinosaurus

1. Was the biggest dinosaur a plant-eater or a meat-eater?
2. Why do you think Argentinosaurus walked on four legs instead of two?
3. How many pounds are in a ton?
4. Look for Argentina on a map. What continent is it on?
5. Do you think Giganotosaurus hunted Argentinosaurus? Why?
6. The modern blue whale weighs about 160 tons. Why do you think dinosaurs didn't grow as large as blue whales?

How big was Tyrannosaurus rex?

Tyrannosaurus (ty-RAN-oh-SAWR-us) rex was about 40 feet long—almost as long as three cars—and weighed about 7 tons, or as much as an African elephant. It had huge jaws and teeth. Some paleontologists think Tyrannosaurus was a *scavenger*. Scavengers eat animals that are already dead. Other scientists believe Tyrannosaurus was a predator that killed its own prey. Tyrannosaurus may have chased down an animal, grasped it with its short, powerful arms, and bit it to death.

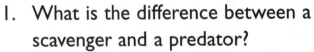

1. What is the difference between a scavenger and a predator?
2. Can you name some living animals that are scavengers?
3. How do scavengers help the *environment*, or nature?
4. How much would three Tyrannosaurus rexes weigh?
5. Tyrannosaurus rex is many people's favorite dinosaur. Why do you think this is?
6. Pretend that you could become any kind of dinosaur for one week. Which dinosaur would you be? Why?

Which dinosaurs were the most fierce?

The fiercest dinosaurs were predators, or meat-eaters. They walked on two legs and had knifelike teeth. Some of the most ferocious dinosaurs were Megalosaurus (MEG-ah-lo-SAWR-us), 30 feet long, from Europe—one of the first large meat-eaters; Allosaurus (AL-oh-SAWR-us), 35 feet long, from North America—had large arms with big claws; Velociraptor (vuh-LOS-ih-RAP-tor), 6 feet long, from Asia—was smart and nimble; Tyrannosaurus (ty-RAN-oh-SAWR-us) rex, 40 feet long, from North America—was among the most powerful dinosaurs.

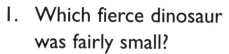

Megalosaurus

1. Which fierce dinosaur was fairly small?
2. What kind of face would you make to look fierce?
3. Do you think human beings are predators? Why?
4. What do you think happened when a meat-eating dinosaur's teeth broke?
5. How do predators help the *environment,* or nature?
6. Some people are *vegetarians,* which means they don't eat meat. If you were a vegetarian, what would you eat?

What were duck-billed dinosaurs?

Hadrosaurs (HAD-ro-sawrs), or duck-billed dinosaurs, were plant-eaters that lived in many parts of the world. They had wide, ducklike mouths and rows of teeth in their cheeks. Scientists believe duckbills were able to make honking or bellowing noises. Different kinds of duckbills had different head ornaments. Some had tall spines, while others had crests or bony lumps. Some had no ornaments at all. Paleontologists think duckbills cared for their young and traveled in herds.

Corythosaurus

Lambeosaurus

1. Why were hadrosaurs called duckbills?
2. What do you think duckbills used their teeth for?

Parasaurolophus

3. What does a honking noise sound like?
4. What does a bellowing noise sound like?
5. What are some head ornaments that modern animals have?

Saurolophus

6. Can you make up some silly dinosaur characters? What are their ears like? What are their mouths like? Draw your dinosaur characters on a separate sheet of paper.

Tsintaosaurus

What were bone-heads?

Pachycephalosaurs (PAK-ih-SEF-ah-lo-sawrs), or bone-heads, were dinosaurs with thick, bony cases around their brains. In some bone-heads, the top of the skull was as round and thick as a bowling ball. Bone-heads probably rammed their heads into enemies, and bumped their heads together when they fought for mates, like sheep and goats do today. Bone-heads were two-legged plant-eaters found in Asia, Madagascar, and North America. They ranged in size from 20 inches to 25 feet.

Pachycephalosaurus

1. Do human beings have bony cases around their brains?
2. *Pachycephalosaur* means "thick-headed lizard." Why do you think scientists chose this name?
3. Find Madagascar on a map or a globe. Which continent is it near?
4. Can you name some things that are harder than bone?
5. What are some living animals that have unusual heads?
6. Who are some people who wear helmets? Why do they wear them?

What were parrot-beaked dinosaurs?

Psittacosaurs (SIT-ah-KO-sawrs), or parrot-beaked dinosaurs, had a long beak at the front of their mouths. Psittacosaurs were plant-eaters, and used their beak and teeth to snip off vegetation. They could not chew well, so they used *gastroliths* (GAS-troh-liths), or stomach stones, to crush food. All known parrot-beaked dinosaurs lived in Asia, and none were longer than about 6 feet. Psittacosaurs are related to dinosaurs that have horns and bony frills around their necks, like Triceratops (try-SAYR-ah-tops).

Psittacosaurus

1. What is another word for **vegetation**?
2. What do you think real parrots use their beaks for?
3. How do you think stones got into dinosaurs' stomachs?
4. Do you think plant-eating dinosaurs or meat-eating dinosaurs had bigger stomachs? Why?
5. Why do birds have different kinds of beaks?
6. Dinosaur frills were often large and fancy. What do you think dinosaurs used them for?

What were long-necks?

Sauropods **(SAWR-oh-pods), or long-necks, were plant-eating dinosaurs with long necks and tails. Found all over the world, long-necks were the largest known dinosaurs. The longest may have been Seismosaurus (SIZE-mo-SAWR-us), from Mexico. Seismosaurus was about 150 feet in length—as long as 10 cars—and weighed around 30 tons, or more than four African elephants. Sauropods walked on four legs and usually had no armor. Scientists think their enormous size and herding habits kept them safe from meat-eaters.**

Seismosaurus

1. Did sauropods travel alone?
2. What modern animals have long necks?
3. Look at a map or a globe. Which U.S. states are closest to Mexico?
4. Can you put these measurements in order, from shortest to longest: 1 yard, 1 foot, 1 inch, 1 mile?
5. What's the longest thing in your room? the shortest thing? About how long are they?
6. Imagine your neck were three times longer than it is. What things would be easier for you to do? What things would be harder?

What kind of dinosaurs were Velociraptors?

Velociraptors (vuh-LOS-ih-RAP-tors) belonged to a group of meat-eating dinosaurs called *dromaeosaurs* (DROH-mee-OH-sawrs). Dromaeosaurs had an enormous curved claw on the second toe of each foot for attacking prey. They also had birdlike skeletons, and paleontologists think they were closely related to birds. Found in Asia, Velociraptor was about 6 feet in length. It was smart, fast, had good eyesight, and may have hunted in packs.

Velociraptor

Thescelosaurus

1. What is happening in the picture?
2. What modern kind of animal is Velociraptor related to?
3. Find Asia on a map or a globe. What are some countries in Asia?
4. How many words can you make up with the letters in **dromaeosaur**?
5. Modern birds of prey, like eagles, are called *raptors*. Can you name some other raptor birds?
6. The movie *Jurassic Park* was about a theme park that contained real, live dinosaurs. Would you like to visit a theme park like this? Why or why not?

What were ostrich dinosaurs?

Ornithomimosaurs (OR-nith-oh-MIME-oh-sawrs) were meat-eating dinosaurs with beaks, small heads, long necks, and long legs. Paleontologists think that ornithomimosaurs looked and ran like ostriches, and sometimes call them *ostrich dinosaurs*. Struthiomimus (STROOTH-ee-oh-MIME-us), an ornithomimosaur from North America, was probably one of the smartest and fastest dinosaurs. It was about 12 feet long and as tall as a human adult.

Struthiomimus

1. Why are ornithomimosaurs called ostrich dinosaurs?
2. Do ostriches have wings? Can they fly?
3. How tall do you think a human adult is?
4. Which do you think could run faster, an ostrich or Struthiomimus?
5. Measure the length of your living room. Was Struthiomimus longer, shorter, or the same length as your living room?
6. If there were a dinosaur called a *zebra dinosaur,* what do you think it would look like? Draw a picture of one on a separate piece of paper.

Are new kinds of dinosaurs still being found?

New kinds of dinosaurs are found all the time. Every year, paleontologists go on *dinosaur digs,* or fossil hunts, in areas that contain sedimentary rocks. Dinosaur digs have recently been done in Africa, Antarctica, Argentina, Canada, China, Madagascar, Mongolia, and the United States. Scientists think there are hundreds of kinds of dinosaurs still to be discovered.

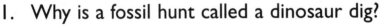

1. Why is a fossil hunt called a dinosaur dig?
2. Two hundred years ago, fossils were called *curiosities.* Why do you think this was?
3. Do you think new kinds of *living* animals are still being discovered?
4. If you could go on a fossil hunt in one of the countries mentioned above, which one would you go to? Why?
5. Besides fossils, what do you think scientists find during a dinosaur dig?
6. *Archaeologists* (AR-kee-OL-uh-jists) study humans who lived a long time ago. What do you think archaeologists look for when they go on archaeology digs?

What were pterosaurs?

Pterosaurs (TAYR-uh-sawrs) were featherless, flying reptiles that lived during the Age of Reptiles. Though distantly related to dinosaurs, pterosaurs were not dinosaurs. Pterosaurs ranged from robin-size creatures to large animals with wingspans of 35 feet. The leathery wings of pterosaurs extended back from rods made of arm and finger bones. When walking, pterosaurs used all four limbs. Pterosaurs probably ate fish and small animals.

Pteranodon

1. What is a wingspan?
2. Some people call pterosaurs "dinosaurs" by mistake. Why do you think they do this?
3. *Pterosaur* means "winged lizard." Why do you think scientists chose this name?
4. How would you tell the difference between a pterosaur and a bird?
5. Can you name some living animals that fly, other than birds?
6. Humans dreamed of flying thousands of years before airplanes were invented. Why do you think people always wanted to fly?

What were plesiosaurs?

Plesiosaurs (PLEE-see-uh-sawrs) were ocean-dwelling reptiles that lived during the Age of Reptiles. They had flippers for swimming and sharp teeth for eating sea creatures. Plesiosaurs ranged in size from about 8 feet to 46 feet—about the length of three cars. Some plesiosaurs had long necks and tiny heads. Others had short necks and big heads. Scientists don't know if plesiosaurs laid eggs on the beach, like sea turtles, or gave birth to live young, like most sharks.

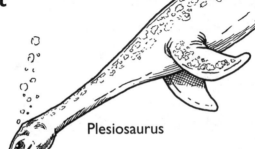

Plesiosaurus

1. How did plesiosaurs swim?
2. How do humans swim?
3. Can you name some modern mammals that live in water?
4. Do you think plesiosaurs breathed with gills or lungs? Why?
5. Reptiles called *ichthyosaurs* (IK-thee-uh-sawrs), or "fish lizards," also lived during the Age of Reptiles. What do you think they were?
6. What is the Loch Ness monster? Do you think it really exists?

What was Archaeopteryx?

Archaeopteryx (AR-kee-OP-tuh-riks) is the oldest known bird. It lived about 150 million years ago, during the Age of Reptiles. Archaeopteryx was about the size of a crow, and had both bird features and dinosaur features. Like a bird, it had wings, feathers, and a beak. Like a dinosaur, it had teeth and a bony tail. Its skeleton was

Archaeopteryx

also similar to some small dinosaur skeletons. Most paleontologists think Archaeopteryx and other birds developed from a dinosaur ancestor and that modern birds are living dinosaurs.

1. How was Archaeopteryx similar to modern birds?
2. How was Archaeopteryx different from modern birds?
3. *Archaeopteryx* means "ancient wing." Why do you think scientists chose this name?
4. What does it mean to "eat like a bird"?
5. Most birds have hollow bones. Why do you think this is?
6. There are many kinds of birds. Can you name some songbirds (birds with musical calls)? some fowl (birds used for food)?

What other kinds of animals lived when dinosaurs lived?

Many kinds of animals were alive during the Mesozoic Era, when dinosaurs flourished. The oceans swarmed with sponges, jellyfish, crabs, shrimps, snails, oysters, corals, sea stars, sea urchins, squids, and fish. The sea also contained swimming reptiles, like plesiosaurs and ichthyosaurs. The land provided homes for insects, spiders, centipedes, salamander-like amphibians, crocodiles, and turtles. Flying reptiles, like pterosaurs, filled the air. Lizards, snakes, small mammals, and birds also appeared during the Mesozoic Era.

Enchodus

1. Can you name some ocean animals that people eat?
2. Which ocean-dwelling animals that lived during the Mesozoic Era had shells?
3. What modern animals are "swimming reptiles"?
4. *Biology* is the study of living things. What do you think *zoology* is?
5. How many kinds of animals do you think live on Earth today?
6. People sometimes develop "new kinds" of dogs, fish, cattle, and so on. Why do you think they do this?

Kuehneosaurus

What are some living relatives of dinosaurs?

All living reptiles, such as turtles, crocodiles, snakes, and lizards, are distantly related to dinosaurs. But the closest relatives of dinosaurs are birds. In fact, most paleontologists believe that *birds are living dinosaurs.* In China, paleontologists recently discovered the fossils of dinosaurs that had feathers but couldn't fly, like Caudipteryx (kaw-DIP-ter-iks). Scientists also discovered an ancient bird that looked like a small flying dinosaur. Scientists think some small dinosaurs developed wings and the ability to fly, and became birds.

Caudipteryx

1. Where were feathered dinosaurs recently discovered?
2. What are the names of some of your relatives?
3. How are these people related to you?
4. Why do some people say dinosaurs didn't really disappear from Earth?
5. What do you think a *bird dog* is?
6. How do scientists figure out which animals are closely related to each other and which aren't?

Why did dinosaurs disappear?

Nobody knows why dinosaurs became *extinct,* or disappeared. But scientists have some *theories,* or ideas. Below are a few of their theories. One or more of these events may have caused dinosaurs to perish.

Asteroid Crash Theory: An asteroid smashed into Earth. The collision created a cloud of dust that surrounded Earth and blocked the Sun. Earth grew cold, and most plants died. Dinosaurs starved and froze.

Volcano Theory: Volcanic eruptions over millions of years produced clouds of dust. The dust blocked the Sun. Earth cooled, and most plants died. Dinosaurs starved and froze.

Climate Theory: Continental movements and shrinking oceans broke up dinosaurs' living areas and made the climate cooler. This led to many dinosaur deaths.

1. What does **perish** mean?
2. Do you think dinosaurs were the only animals on Earth that became extinct?

3. Some scientists say the Earth's climate is getting warmer. Do you think a warmer climate would cause some animals to become extinct?

4. Why do different scientists have different theories about dinosaur extinction?

5. If an asteroid were heading straight for Earth, what could scientists do to prevent a collision?

6. Do you think dinosaurs will ever appear on Earth again? Why or why not?

One Step Further

Make a *diorama,* or three-dimensional scene, showing the extinction of the dinosaurs. Get a shoebox, construction paper, old magazines, markers or crayons, scissors, and glue. Choose one or more of the extinction theories described on page 56. Cut out pictures of dinosaurs, plants, an asteroid, volcanoes, and so on from old magazines, or draw them on construction paper. Glue the pictures into the shoebox to create a scene that shows the end of the dinosaur age. For example, you could show an asteroid crater, volcanoes erupting, a cloud of dust blocking out the Sun, dead plants, and dying dinosaurs.

Why did mammals get bigger after dinosaurs became extinct?

On Earth, each kind of animal has its own *niche* (NITCH), or place in nature. An animal's niche depends on many things, including where it lives and what it eats. During the Mesozoic Era, dinosaurs took up most of the land niches. They lived almost everywhere and ate almost everything. When dinosaurs disappeared, their niches became available. Mammals could then develop into new, larger forms, like the mammoth, and take over these niches.

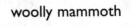

woolly mammoth

1. What is an animal's niche?
2. How is a parrot's niche different from a lion's niche?
3. How is a woolly mammoth like an elephant? How is it different?
4. What are some living mammals that were not around during the Age of Reptiles?
5. What are some features of mammals?
6. If a disaster killed off most mammals on Earth, which animals do you think would take over their niches? Why?

Why are people so interested in dinosaurs?

People are interested in dinosaurs because dinosaurs looked like dragons and monsters—*but they were real.* People are fascinated by the huge, knifelike teeth and slashing claws of Tyrannosaurus (ty-RAN-oh-SAWR-us), the showy armor of Ankylosaurus (ANG-kih-loh-SAWR-us), the frills and horns of Triceratops (try-SAYR-ah-tops), and the gigantic body of Brachiosaurus (BRAK-ee-oh-SAWR-us). People wonder what it was like to live in the world of dinosaurs, and why dinosaurs disappeared.

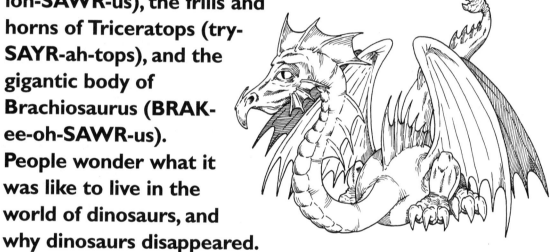

1. Why are you interested in dinosaurs?
2. Which dinosaur is your favorite? Why?
3. How would you describe a dragon?
4. A dragon is one kind of monster. What are some other monsters?
5. Do you like scary things, like monster movies, horror stories, and spooky television shows? Why or why not?
6. Other than family and friends, what are your 10 favorite things in the world?

Answers

Page 5

1. Reptiles lay eggs, and have backbones, lungs, and scaly skin.
2. Sample answers: Turtles, lizards, snakes, crocodiles, and alligators.
3. Answers will vary.
4. Sample answers: Humans, dogs, cats, horses, and birds.
5. Sample answers: Legs under your body keep you higher above the ground, so you can step over rocks and other obstacles more easily; you can run faster.
6. Answers will vary.

Page 6

1. Frogs and salamanders.
2. It means having lived a very long time ago.
3. They developed stronger skeletons, tougher skins, and hard eggs.
4. Scientists think amphibians came from ancient fish that developed lungs and strong fins, and crawled onto land.
5. Sample answers: Nap, map, man, ham, hip, pin, pan, and pain.
6. Sample answer: In some ways, it's easier to live in water. Water helps support an animal's weight, and swimming requires less energy than walking. For people, however, it's easier to live on land. People have legs for walking and lungs to breathe air.

Page 7

1. The Ornithischia.
2. Parent: Child should point to his or her hips.
3. The Saurischia.
4. Sample answers: Horses, cows, elephants, giraffes, rabbits, squirrels, and deer.
5. Sample answers: Dogs, cats, tigers, lions, crocodiles, owls, and sharks.
6. Sample answer: Humans are more like birds because they both have two legs and are warm-blooded.

Pages 8–9

1. Because he was a fossil collector.
2. Sample answer: Teeth from meat-eaters might look like giant dog teeth; teeth from plant-eaters might look like giant horse teeth.
3. Teeth marks on dinosaur bones may be from predators that bit the dinosaurs, or from scavengers that chewed on the bones.
4. Dinosaur bones and teeth resembled lizard bones and teeth, and no one had heard of dinosaurs at that time.
5. Answers will vary.
6. Sample answers: Some people are curious; some want to be rich and famous; some want to have adventures; and some want to bring honor to their country.

Page 10

1. No. Paleontologists study many different plants and animals.
2. Each wanted to be the first to discover new dinosaurs.
3. Plant fossils include preserved seeds, and marks left by branches and leaves.
4. Sample answers: Hammers and chisels to pry fossils out of rocks; brushes for removing loose rock and dirt; measuring tape to measure fossil sites; and plaster to make the fossil jackets.
5. Sample answers: So they know how to get back to the area; so they can re-create the dinosaur world.
6. Answers will vary.

Page 11

1. Answers will vary.
2. In the year 2000, 1842 was 158 years ago.
3. Answers will vary.
4. In the 1800s, people didn't know what dinosaurs looked like, so they assumed they looked like mammals.
5. Dinosaur bones were often scattered around by animals or flowing water before they became fossils. As a result, scientists don't always know which skull goes with which body.
6. Answers will vary.

Page 12

1. The Mesozoic Era, when dinosaurs lived.
2. Scientists think the first dinosaurs were small animals that ate insects and other small creatures. Large dinosaurs appeared later.
3. 180 million years (subtract 65 from 245).
4. It means dinosaurs existed during prehistoric times, before humans began recording, or writing down, history.
5. Because many new kinds of mammals have appeared during this era.
6. Answers will vary.

Page 13

1. Pangaea was a supercontinent made up of all the landmasses on Earth.
2. A "superocean" surrounded Pangaea. Scientists named the huge ocean Panthalassa (PAN-thah-LASS-ah).
3. There are seven continents: Africa, Antarctica, Asia, Australia, Europe, North America, and South America.
4. Asia is the largest continent and Australia is the smallest.
5. The continents are moving now. For example, North and South America are moving away from Europe and Africa, and toward Asia. The motion is very slow and not very noticeable.
6. Different parts of Pangaea had different weather conditions. Areas close to the equator were hotter than areas far from the equator; wind patterns and mountain ranges caused some places to get more rainfall than others. This is similar to what happens on Earth today.

Page 14

1. The climate was warm.
2. Answers will vary. If the child lives in a warm climate, dinosaurs would probably do well.
3. No, the poles were not covered with ice because the climate was too warm.
4. Different plants grow in different climates. As plants evolved, or changed over time, they developed features that suited their environment. For example, cactuses developed thick stems that store water, so they can live in hot, dry climates. Spruce trees developed the ability to survive cold temperatures, so they can live in cool, northern climates.
5. A habitat is the environment, or place, where a person, an animal, or a plant lives and grows.
6. Sample answer: When animals eat fruits, the seeds pass through their bodies and come out in their stools. As animals move around, the seeds spread to new places.

Page 15

1. No, because there were no people during the dinosaur age.
2. An ancestor is a person (or animal) related to us who lived a long time ago. Rest of answer will vary.
3. They ate insects, fruits, and small animals.
4. Baboons, gorillas, and orangutans are primates.
5. Sample answers: Knock fruit off trees; get termites from their nest (to eat them).
6. Sample answers: Modern humans have large brains and great intelligence; they use tools and language; and they can adapt to many different environments.

Pages 16–17

1. It means to keep something from being damaged; to prevent it from decomposing or decaying.
2. No. Fossils are the remains of plants and animals that lived millions of years ago.
3. It depends on the size of the fossil. It often takes years to remove an entire dinosaur skeleton from the surrounding rock. Scientists work slowly and carefully so they won't damage the bones.
4. They match the size and shape of the footprints with bones from dinosaur feet.
5. From the size of the droppings, scientists can estimate how large the dinosaur was and how much it ate. From the contents of the droppings (bits of plants or bits of bone), scientists can figure out what the dinosaur ate.
6. Answers will vary.

Page 18

1. Sample answers: A natural history museum; a dinosaur exhibition.
2. They were probably washed into rivers and lakes by heavy rainstorms and floods.
3. Sandstone is made of bits of sand "cemented" together to form rock.
4. If the bones weren't covered with sediments, they would have been chewed up by animals or destroyed by weather (sun, rain, and wind).
5. Sediments are covering the dinosaur's body. If the body becomes covered with layers of sediment and the layers harden into rock, the dinosaur's bones will become fossils.
6. Sample answer: Scientists go to places with sedimentary rocks of the right age. They bring animal experts, plant experts, and extra people to help dig. They take extra clothes, tents, food, digging equipment, cameras, and so on.

Page 19

1. Latin and Greek.
2. Answers will vary.
3. Alberta.
4. New Mexico borders Arizona, Colorado, Oklahoma, and Texas.
5. No. Once an animal gets an official scientific name, the name is used all over the world.
6. Answers will vary.

Pages 20–21

1. Animals with backbones.
2. Answers will vary.
3. Sample answers: Worms, jellyfish, spiders, lobsters, and sea stars.
4. Paleontologists use glue, rods, and wire to attach the bones together.

5. Sample answers: Large dinosaurs were safe from most meat-eaters, but they had to find huge amounts of food. Small dinosaurs could run fast and hide easily, but they might be attacked by big dinosaurs.
6. Scientists study other dinosaurs and modern animals to figure out what the missing bones looked like. Then they make artificial bones—from strong, light materials—to fill in the gaps.

Page 22

1. They can learn where muscles were attached and how big they were.
2. Leg muscles are generally larger than arm muscles in humans, because legs are longer and stronger.
3. Wrist joints.
4. They needed to be strong so they wouldn't break.
5. Muscles are soft tissues. They usually break down soon after an animal dies, and rarely form fossils.
6. Soft-bodied animals, such as jellyfish and worms, almost never form fossils because their bodies break down too quickly after they die.

Page 23

1. Dinosaur skin impressions are sometimes preserved in rocks.
2. Sample answers: Shoes, boots, jackets, handbags, and clothes are often made of leather, which is produced from the skin of animals such as cattle, goats, and sheep.
3. Plant-eaters were more likely to be attacked by predators. Their tougher skin helped to protect them from teeth and claws.
4. It means that water cannot enter or escape.
5. Waterproof skin keeps their bodies from drying out.
6. Sample answers: Peacocks use their colorful tails to attract mates; bumblebees' black and yellow stripes warn enemies; tigers' stripes help them hide in tall grass.

Pages 24–25

1. The bird, a warm-blooded animal, would be more active. The frog would not be able to absorb much heat from cold surroundings.
2. Sample answers: Warm-blooded animals—all mammals and birds, such as monkeys, dogs, elephants, ostriches, and owls. Cold-blooded animals—all fish, frogs, salamanders, turtles, and snakes.
3. The body processes of warm-blooded animals require more energy than those of cold-blooded animals. The energy is supplied by food.

4. Cold-blooded animals are able to be more active in a warm climate than in a cold climate.
5. Sample answers: Bears, ground squirrels, bats, and toads.
6. *Ectotherms* are cold-blooded animals. *Ectotherm* means "heat from outside."

One Step Further: The large potato feels warmer because large objects cool more slowly than small objects.

Page 26

1. Meat-eating dinosaurs.
2. Most children have 20 teeth.
3. Sample answer: Leave it under the pillow for the tooth fairy.
4. Dogs are meat-eaters; they have sharp teeth to tear up meat. Horses are plant-eaters; they have grinding teeth to chew up plants. Humans eat meat and plants; they have some sharp teeth and some grinding teeth.
5. To mash it up, so you can swallow it easily. A large, unchewed piece of food could get stuck in your throat and cause you to choke.
6. You would probably have to tranquilize the animals, to keep them from being bitten. You'd need large tools for the tiger, and tiny tools for the bat.

Page 27

1. Because some had large brains compared to their body size.
2. Dinosaurs were not as smart as people; their brains weren't large enough.
3. Sample answers: Gorillas, chimpanzees, whales, dolphins, and elephants.
4. Sample answers: Meat-eating baby dinosaurs may have learned how to hunt; plant-eating baby dinosaurs may have learned which plants were best to eat.
5. Sample answers: Go to school, study, and read lots of books.
6. Answers will vary.

Page 28

1. It means *thin* or *narrow*.
2. Sample answers: Giraffes, ostriches, storks, and cranes.
3. Many animals have short necks. Sample answers: Elephants, gorillas, pigs, and owls.
4. No. Humans usually stop growing when they're young adults.
5. Answers will vary.
6. Scientists believe long-necks probably lived on firm, dry ground, where they could walk around easily. Such heavy animals would have sunk into muddy ground and got stuck.

Page 29

1. The Ankylosaurus is using its clublike tail to defend itself from an attacking predator.

2. Paleontologists think horns may have been used to stab attacking predators, or to fight for mates, or both.
3. Sample answers: Rhinoceroses, moose, bighorn sheep, deer, and antelope.
4. Sample answers: Armadillos, turtles, and tortoises.
5. Armor suits protected knights from the spears, arrows, and swords of their enemies.
6. They probably hid or ran away.

Page 30
1. Some dinosaurs had whiplike tails, to lash out at predators. Others had clubs or spikes on their tails, to smash into predators.
2. Without long tails to balance their bodies, dinosaurs would have been "front heavy," and would have fallen forward on their faces.
3. Crocodiles use their tails to swim and to strike out at enemies.
4. Unlike a crocodile's tail, a monkey's tail can wrap around things. Monkeys use their tails to swing from tree to tree.
5. It helps to steer the plane.
6. A *tail* is a part that extends from the rear end of an animal or object. A *tale* is a story.

Page 31
1. To catch and eat food.
2. Sample answers: Lions, tigers, eagles, hawks, and lobsters.
3. Human fingernails and toenails are most similar to dinosaur claws.
4. Sample answers: Sharks and some snakes catch prey with their teeth; squid and octopuses catch prey with their tentacles.
5. In the state of Utah.
6. Answers will vary.

Page 32
1. No. Some had better smell than vision.
2. By wearing glasses or contact lenses, or by having laser surgery to correct their vision.
3. Elephants use their trunks to smell. This helps them find food and detect enemies.
4. Sample answers: Cats, owls, and some bats.
5. Hearing, touch, taste, and smell.
6. To learn about their surroundings and what's happening around them.

Page 33
1. An echo is a repeated sound. Rest of answer will vary.
2. Sample answers: Baby dinosaurs may have squealed when they were scared or hurt, or to get food from their parents.

3. Sample answers: Adult dinosaurs may have made noises to attract mates, scare away enemies, or warn each other about predators.
4. Sample answers: A lion roars, a wolf howls, and a snake hisses.
5. Dinosaurs with good hearing may have been able to locate their prey from a great distance, or when it was too dark to see well.
6. Answers will vary.

Page 34
1. On the ground.
2. Many dinosaurs were too big and heavy to sit on their eggs. The eggs would have broken.
3. Sample answers: Birds, fish, frogs, turtles, and snakes.
4. Sample answer: Mammals—such as humans, dogs, cats, and hamsters—give birth to live young. Rest of answer will vary.
5. Sample answers: Fried, scrambled, hard-boiled, and poached. A large dinosaur egg could probably serve a hundred people or more.
6. They learn how big baby dinosaurs were, how they grew, and what they looked like.

Page 35
1. The mother dinosaur is licking one of her newly hatched babies.
2. Sample answers: By feeding you, keeping you warm, changing your diapers, and keeping you safe from danger.
3. Because Maiasaura nests suggest these dinosaurs were probably "good mothers" who took care of their babies.
4. Sample answers: Pup, kitten, cub, calf, chick, piglet, fawn, joey, and tadpole.
5. Answers will vary.
6. Sample answers: Feed your babies, keep them warm, teach them how to hunt or find plants to eat, and protect them from other dinosaurs.

Page 36
1. Answers will vary.
2. Scientists think plant-eaters were more likely to live in groups, to protect themselves from predators.
3. Sample answers: Elephants, lions, wolves, sheep, dolphins, geese, and bees.
4. Sample answers: Pack (of wolves), pride (of lions), flock (of sheep or birds), swarm (of bees), and school (of fish).
5. Scientists think this may mean that the dinosaur families, adults and young, traveled together.
6. Answers will vary.

Page 37
1. To have a steady supply of food.

2. To move to warmer climates where there is more food available.
3. Scientists believe migrating animals are guided by "clues" such as the Sun and stars, the Earth's magnetic field, chemical smells, and inborn knowledge of where to go.
4. Maps help people find their way around when they travel. A map shows the roads, mountains, rivers, parks, and landmarks of a specific area.
5. Sample answers: Because it got too hot or too cold; there was too much or too little rain; there were volcanic eruptions or earthquakes; food ran out; or they were chased away by other tribes.
6. Answers will vary.

Pages 38–39
1. To flee from predators or to chase prey.
2. No, you couldn't. The fastest humans can only run about 20 miles per hour.
3. Sample answers: Cheetahs, gazelles, horses, greyhounds, jackrabbits, and ostriches.
4. 15 miles.
5. Snails have shells and sea urchins have spines. These help protect them from enemies.
6. Other words for *fast* are *quick, swift, speedy,* and *rapid.* Rest of answer will vary.
One Step Further: Your stride gets longer when you run.

Page 40
1. Probably. Compsognathus weighed only about 7 pounds.
2. Because Heterodontosaurus had several different kinds of teeth.
3. Answers will vary.
4. Sample answers: Little, tiny, puny, miniature, petite, and peewee.
5–6. Answers will vary.

Page 41
1. A plant-eater—Argentinosaurus.
2. It had to walk on four legs to support its great weight.
3. 2,000.
4. Argentina is in South America.
5. Scientists think most huge dinosaurs, like Argentinosaurus, were too big to be hunted by predators. A group of meat-eaters, however, may have been able to kill one.
6. The blue whale lives in water, which helps support its enormous body. If dinosaurs grew as large as blue whales, their bones might have collapsed from the enormous weight they carried.

Page 42
1. A scavenger eats animals that are already dead. A predator kills its own prey.

2. Sample answers: Hyenas, vultures, and seagulls.
3. By getting rid of dead animals, which might rot, smell, and cause diseases.
4. 21 tons.
5–6. Answers will vary.

Page 43
1. Velociraptor.
2. Answers will vary.
3. Yes, because human beings kill animals to eat.
4. The dinosaur quickly grew new teeth.
5. By controlling the number of plant-eaters in an area. If there were no predators, plant-eaters would kill off the plants and then they would starve.
6. Answers will vary.

Page 44
1. Because they had wide, ducklike mouths.
2. To chew plants.
3. *Parent: Child should imitate a honking sound.*
4. *Parent: Child should imitate a bellowing sound.*
5. Sample answers: Goats have horns, moose have antlers, and some birds have crests.
6. Answers will vary.

Page 45
1. Yes. The bony case around the human brain is the skull.
2. Because bone-heads have thick, heavy skulls.
3. Africa.
4. Sample answers: Diamonds, granite rocks, and steel tools (hammers, axes).
5. Sample answers: Aardvarks (long, thin snout), hammerhead sharks (hammer-shaped head), moose (huge antlers), and snails (eyes on stalks).
6. Sample answers: Football players, hockey players, cyclists, motorcycle drivers, race car drivers, and soldiers. People wear helmets to protect their heads from injury.

Page 46
1. Sample answers: Plants, greenery, and foliage.
2. To climb through trees, open seeds, and eat fruit.
3. The dinosaurs swallowed the stones.
4. Plant-eaters had bigger stomachs. Plants are less nutritious than meat, so plant-eaters had to eat more.
5. To get different kinds of food. For example, woodpeckers peck at tree trunks to find bugs, pelicans catch fish, and hummingbirds drink nectar from flowers.

6. Scientists think some dinosaurs used their frills to attract mates, to scare off rivals, and to protect themselves from enemies.

Page 47
1. No. Scientists believe sauropods lived and moved in herds.
2. Sample answers: Giraffes, swans, cranes, herons, and storks.
3. California, Arizona, New Mexico, and Texas are closest to Mexico.
4. 1 inch, 1 foot, 1 yard, 1 mile.
5–6. Answers will vary.

Page 48
1. A Velociraptor is attacking a larger dinosaur using the curved claw on its foot.
2. Birds.
3. Sample answers: Russia, China, Mongolia, India, Korea, Japan, Thailand, Vietnam, Iran, and Iraq.
4. Sample answers: Drum, door, red, road, rode, made, moss, arm, and sour.
5. Sample answers: Owls, hawks, falcons, and vultures.
6. Answers will vary.

Page 49
1. Because ornithomimosaurs looked and ran like ostriches.
2. Ostriches do have wings, but they can't fly.
3. The average height of human adults is about 5½ feet.
4. An ostrich. Ostriches can run about 40 miles per hour. Scientists think Struthiomimus could run about 35 miles per hour.
5. Answers will vary.
6. It would have black and white stripes. Rest of answer will vary.

Page 50
1. Because paleontologists dig dinosaur bones out of rocks.
2. Because people didn't know what they were and were *curious* about them.
3. Yes. Giant tube worms and other animals were discovered on the bottom of the ocean in 1979, and new insects are found every year. Occasionally, a new vertebrate is discovered.
4. Answers will vary.
5. They uncover dinosaur nests, eggs, stomach stones, droppings, and footprints.
6. They look for ancient buildings, houses, cave dwellings, clothes, tools, jewelry, weapons, writings, drawings, burial sites, human bones, and many other things.

Page 51
1. It is the distance from one wing tip to the other, when a pair of wings are fully extended.
2. Because both pterosaurs and dinosaurs were reptiles that lived a long time ago.
3. Because pterosaurs were reptiles with wings.
4. Birds have feathers and pterosaurs didn't.
5. Insects and bats.
6. Answers will vary.

Page 52
1. With their flippers.
2. With their arms and legs.
3. Sample answers: Whales, dolphins, and seals.
4. Plesiosaurs had lungs. They breathed air, like all reptiles.
5. Ichthyosaurs were reptiles that looked and swam like fish. They were shaped like modern dolphins.
6. The Loch Ness monster is supposedly a large, dinosaur-like creature that lives in Loch Ness, a lake in Scotland. Rest of answer will vary.

Page 53
1. It had wings, feathers, and a beak.
2. It had teeth and a bony tail, and a skeleton similar to those of some small dinosaurs.
3. Because Archaeopteryx was the oldest known bird.
4. It means to eat very little food.
5. Hollow bones reduce their weight, making it easier for them to fly.
6. Sample answers: Songbirds—nightingales, bluebirds, canaries, mockingbirds, robins, and cardinals. Fowl—chickens, ducks, geese, and turkeys.

Page 54
1. Sample answers: Fish, lobsters, shrimps, crabs, oysters, clams, octopuses, and squids.
2. Crabs, shrimps, snails, and oysters.
3. Sample answers: Sea turtles, crocodiles, alligators, sea snakes, and marine iguanas.
4. Zoology is the study of animals.
5. No one knows. Scientists have named at least 1½ million animals so far, and there are probably many more.
6. Because they want animals with certain features; for example, miniature (small) dogs; pretty fish with long fins; and cows that give extra milk.

Page 55
1. In China.
2–3. Answers will vary.
4. Because birds are still alive, and they believe birds are dinosaurs.
5. A bird dog is a dog that helps hunters locate birds that they've shot.

6. Scientists study animals' appearance (how they look), behavior, growth, reproduction, genetic material (DNA), and other features. Animals that are more similar to each other are usually more closely related.

Pages 56–57

1. It means to die.
2. No. Many kinds of animals have become extinct since life began on Earth.
3. It probably would. A major change in climate always causes some animals to become extinct.
4. Because no single theory can be proven at the present time.
5. Sample answer: Send up a rocket filled with explosives. A huge explosion might push the asteroid out of the way or blast it apart.

6. It's very unlikely that dinosaurs will ever reappear on Earth. No extinct animals have ever come back.

Page 58

1. Its place in nature. A niche includes where the animal lives and what it eats.
2. Parrots live in trees and eat fruits and nuts. Lions live on the ground and kill other animals for food.
3. Sample answers: Like—Both are large animals with four legs, a trunk, and two tusks. Different—A woolly mammoth has long hair and an elephant does not; a mammoth's tusks are longer and more rounded.
4. Sample answers: Horses, dogs, cats, monkeys, apes, tigers, lions, seals, and whales.

5. Mammals are warm-blooded, have hair, and produce milk to feed their babies. Most give birth to live young.
6. Answers will vary. (There is no incorrect answer.)

Page 59

1–3. Answers will vary.
4. Sample answers: Vampires, werewolves, zombies, Frankenstein, and the bogeyman.
5–6. Answers will vary.